I0620192

Success

Unleash Your Potential and Transform Your Life with the Proven Strategies and Techniques for Achieving Success: The Ultimate Guide to Personal Growth and Fulfillment

Lance P. Richards

Success: Unleash Your Potential and Transform Your Life with the Proven Strategies and Techniques for Achieving Success: The Ultimate Guide to Personal Growth and Fulfillment

Table of Contents

01: Introduction: Defining Success

Success is a word that is used frequently in our daily lives, but it means something different to everyone. Some people define success as wealth and material possessions, while others define it as happiness, personal fulfillment, or a sense of purpose. The truth is, success is a highly personal and subjective concept, and what it means to you will depend on your individual values, beliefs, and goals.

Success is not just about achieving your goals, but it's also about the journey to get there. It's about the person you become along the way and the impact you have on the world around you. Success is not just about what you achieve, but it's also about who you are and the way you live your life.

For this reason, success is not just about reaching your destination, but it's also about the journey to get there. Success is not just a destination, but a journey filled with growth, learning, and discovery. The journey to success is not just about reaching your goals, but it's also about the person you become along the way.

The purpose of this book is to provide you with the

strategies and techniques you need to unleash your potential and transform your life. The ultimate goal of this guide is to help you achieve success on your own terms and live the life you have always dreamed of. Whether you're seeking personal fulfillment, financial stability, or a sense of purpose, this book will provide you with the tools and techniques you need to succeed.

In the following chapters, we will explore the key elements of success, including goal setting, self-confidence, positive thinking, emotional intelligence, time management, and much more. We will also delve into topics such as entrepreneurship, leadership, financial management, and creativity, providing you with the strategies and techniques you need to achieve success in all areas of your life.

So, are you ready to start your journey to success? If so, let's get started!

02: Understanding Your Mindset: The Key to Unlocking Your Potential

Your mindset is a powerful tool that has the ability to shape your life and determine your success. It is the set of beliefs, attitudes, and assumptions that you hold about yourself, others, and the world around you. Your mindset influences your thoughts, emotions, and actions, and it has a profound impact on your ability to achieve your goals and live the life you want.

There are two main types of mindsets: a fixed mindset and a growth mindset. People with a fixed mindset believe that their abilities, intelligence, and talents are set in stone and cannot be changed. They are often afraid of failure and are less likely to take risks or embrace challenges. On the other hand, people with a growth mindset believe that their abilities and intelligence can be developed and improved over time. They embrace challenges as opportunities for growth and are more likely to persevere in the face of setbacks.

Research has shown that people with a growth mindset are more successful in all areas of their lives, including their careers, relationships, and personal development. They are more confident, optimistic, and resilient, and they are better equipped to handle the challenges and obstacles that come their way.

So, how can you develop a growth mindset and unlock your potential? Here are some tips:

– Embrace challenges: Instead of viewing challenges as obstacles, view them as opportunities for growth and learning. This will help you develop a positive outlook on life and increase your resilience in the face of setbacks.

– Cultivate a love of learning: Seek out new experiences, challenge yourself to learn new skills, and embrace the process of growth and development.

– Practice gratitude: Focus on what you have, not what you don't have. Cultivate an attitude of gratitude and be thankful for the blessings in your life.

– Surround yourself with positive people: Surround yourself with people who encourage and support you. Seek out mentors who can help guide you on your journey to success.

02: UNDERSTANDING YOUR MINDSET: THE KEY TO UNLOCKING YOUR POTENTIAL

– Embrace failure: Embrace failure as a learning opportunity and use it as a catalyst for growth. Don't be afraid to take risks and make mistakes, as they are essential to your growth and development.

By developing a growth mindset and embracing challenges, you will be able to unlock your full potential and achieve success in all areas of your life. So, take the time to cultivate a positive outlook and embrace the journey to success. The rewards will be immeasurable!

03: Setting SMART Goals: Define Your Path to Success

Goals are the foundation of success. They provide direction, motivation, and a sense of purpose, and they help you stay focused on what you want to achieve. However, not all goals are created equal. In order to be effective, goals must be specific, measurable, attainable, relevant, and time-bound. This is where the concept of SMART goals comes in.

SMART is an acronym that stands for Specific, Measurable, Attainable, Relevant, and Time-Bound. The following are the key components of SMART goals:

– Specific: Your goals should be clear, specific, and well defined. They should answer the questions of what, why, and how.

– Measurable: Your goals should be quantifiable, so you can track your progress and know when you have achieved them.

– Attainable: Your goals should be realistic and achievable, given your current resources and circumstances.

– Relevant: Your goals should be relevant to your values,

beliefs, and personal or professional goals.

– Time-bound: Your goals should have a deadline, so you can focus your efforts and stay motivated to achieve them.

When you set SMART goals, you are more likely to achieve them, because you have a clear plan and a roadmap to follow. Here are some steps to help you set effective SMART goals:

– Identify your desires and values: Take the time to reflect on what is important to you and what you truly want to achieve in life.

– Write down your goals: Write down your goals and be as specific as possible. Use the SMART criteria to help you.

– Prioritize your goals: Rank your goals in order of priority, so you can focus your efforts and stay on track.

– Break down your goals: Break down your goals into smaller, more manageable steps, so you can make steady progress towards your ultimate goal.

– Create a plan of action: Write down a plan of action, including specific tasks and deadlines, so you can stay focused and motivated.

– Review and adjust your goals: Regularly review your goals and make any necessary adjustments. Celebrate your achievements and stay focused on your ultimate goal.

Setting SMART goals is an important step in the journey to success. By defining your goals and creating a clear plan of action, you will be able to focus your efforts, stay motivated, and achieve the success you desire. So, take the time to set effective SMART goals and start your journey to success today!

04: Overcoming Limiting Beliefs and Negative Thoughts

Your thoughts and beliefs play a crucial role in determining your success in life. If you have negative beliefs and thoughts, you are likely to limit your potential and hold yourself back from achieving your goals. However, the good news is that you can overcome these limiting beliefs and negative thoughts with the right strategies and techniques.

Limiting beliefs are defined as beliefs that hold you back and prevent you from achieving your goals. They can be based on past experiences, societal expectations, or cultural norms, and they can take many different forms. Examples of limiting beliefs include "I'm not good enough," "I can't do it," "I'm not worthy," or "I'm not smart enough."

Negative thoughts, on the other hand, are thoughts that are negative in nature and can have a significant impact on your emotions and behavior. Negative thoughts can include self-criticism, worry, fear, or doubt. They can also be linked to limiting beliefs and can reinforce them.

The first step in overcoming limiting beliefs and negative thoughts is to identify them. This requires a level of self-awareness and introspection, so you can understand what you believe and what thoughts are holding you back. Once you have identified your limiting beliefs and negative thoughts, you can start to challenge and change them.

There are several strategies and techniques you can use to overcome limiting beliefs and negative thoughts, including:

– Mindfulness: Mindfulness is the practice of being present and aware in the moment. By focusing on your thoughts and emotions, you can gain a better understanding of what you believe and what thoughts are holding you back.

– Affirmations: Affirmations are positive statements that you can use to replace limiting beliefs and negative thoughts. By repeating affirmations regularly, you can start to believe in them and change your thoughts and beliefs.

– Cognitive behavioral therapy (CBT): CBT is a type of therapy that focuses on changing negative thoughts and beliefs. By working with a therapist, you can learn how to identify and challenge negative thoughts and beliefs, and replace them with more positive and empowering ones.

04: OVERCOMING LIMITING BELIEFS AND NEGATIVE THOUGHTS

– Visualization: Visualization is the practice of creating mental images of your goals and desires. By visualizing your future, you can start to believe in your potential and overcome limiting beliefs and negative thoughts.

– Surrounding yourself with positive influences: Surrounding yourself with positive influences can help you overcome limiting beliefs and negative thoughts. This includes spending time with positive and supportive people, reading positive books and articles, and engaging in activities that bring you joy and fulfillment.

By using these strategies and techniques, you can start to overcome your limiting beliefs and negative thoughts, and unleash your full potential. Remember, changing your thoughts and beliefs takes time and effort, but it is worth it. With the right tools and a positive attitude, you can achieve anything you set your mind to.

05: Building Self-Confidence: Take Control of Your Life

Self-confidence is a critical component of success and personal growth. It is the belief in yourself and your abilities, and it allows you to take control of your life and achieve your goals. Without self-confidence, it can be difficult to take risks, step outside of your comfort zone, and reach your full potential.

Fortunately, self-confidence is something that can be developed and strengthened with practice and effort. By using the right strategies and techniques, you can build self-confidence and take control of your life.

Here are some of the most effective ways to build self-confidence:

− Identify and challenge negative self-talk: Negative self-talk can have a significant impact on your self-confidence. By identifying and challenging these negative thoughts, you can start to replace them with more positive and empowering ones.

− Practice self-care: Taking care of your physical, emotional, and mental well-being is essential for building self-confidence. By engaging in activities that bring you joy and fulfillment, you can boost your self-esteem and feel better about yourself.

– Set and achieve small goals: Setting and achieving small goals can help you build self-confidence by giving you a sense of accomplishment. Start with simple goals, such as reading a book, learning a new skill, or going for a walk, and work your way up to more challenging goals as you feel more confident.

– Surround yourself with positive influences: Spending time with positive and supportive people can help you build self-confidence. By surrounding yourself with individuals who believe in you and your abilities, you can start to believe in yourself too.

– Embrace failure: Failure is a natural part of the journey towards success, and it can help you build self-confidence by teaching you resilience and perseverance. Embrace failure as an opportunity to learn and grow, and don't be afraid to take risks.

05: BUILDING SELF-CONFIDENCE: TAKE CONTROL OF YOUR LIFE

– Practice positive self-talk: Positive self-talk is a powerful tool for building self-confidence. By speaking kindly and positively to yourself, you can start to believe in yourself and your abilities.

– Focus on your strengths: Rather than focusing on your weaknesses, focus on your strengths and the things that you are good at. This will help you build self-confidence by reminding you of what you are capable of.

Building self-confidence takes time and effort, but it is a critical component of success and personal growth. By using these strategies and techniques, you can take control of your life and unleash your full potential. Remember, confidence is not something that you are born with, but something that you can develop with the right tools and mindset.

06: Developing a Positive Mental Attitude: Harnessing the Power of Optimism

Your mental attitude has a significant impact on your success and overall well-being. A positive mental attitude can help you overcome challenges, remain optimistic in the face of adversity, and achieve your goals. On the other hand, a negative mental attitude can hold you back, causing you to feel discouraged and defeated.

Developing a positive mental attitude takes effort and dedication, but it is a critical component of success and personal growth. By harnessing the power of optimism, you can transform your life and achieve your full potential.

Here are some strategies for developing a positive mental attitude:

– Practice gratitude: Gratitude is a powerful tool for developing a positive mental attitude. By focusing on what you are grateful for, you can shift your perspective from negative to positive and cultivate an optimistic outlook.

– Surround yourself with positive influences: Spending time

with positive and supportive people can help you develop a positive mental attitude. By surrounding yourself with individuals who bring out the best in you, you can start to adopt their positive outlook.

– Focus on the present moment: When you are focused on the present moment, you can avoid dwelling on the past or worrying about the future. This can help you develop a positive mental attitude and remain optimistic, even in challenging situations.

– Reframe negative thoughts: When negative thoughts arise, try to reframe them in a positive light. For example, instead of thinking, "I'll never be able to do this," try thinking, "I may not be able to do this yet, but I can learn and improve."

– Engage in physical activity: Exercise has been shown to have a positive impact on mental well-being and can help you develop a positive mental attitude. Whether it's taking a walk, practicing yoga, or playing a sport, engaging in physical activity can help you feel more optimistic and energized.

06: DEVELOPING A POSITIVE MENTAL ATTITUDE: HARNESSING THE POWER OF OPTIMISM

– Practice mindfulness: Mindfulness is a powerful tool for developing a positive mental attitude. By focusing on the present moment and your breath, you can cultivate inner peace and positivity, even in the face of stress and adversity.

– Embrace change: Change can be difficult, but it is a natural part of life. By embracing change and viewing it as an opportunity for growth and learning, you can develop a positive mental attitude and remain optimistic even in the face of uncertainty.

A positive mental attitude is essential for success and personal growth. By using these strategies and techniques, you can harness the power of optimism and transform your life. Remember, your mental attitude is a choice, and you have the power to cultivate positivity and optimism in your life.

07: Enhancing Your Emotional Intelligence: Connecting with Others and Yourself

Emotional intelligence is the ability to understand and manage your emotions, as well as the emotions of others. It plays a crucial role in success and personal growth, as it helps you navigate relationships, communicate effectively, and make better decisions.

By enhancing your emotional intelligence, you can improve your relationships, boost your self-awareness, and become more resilient in the face of challenges. Here are some strategies for enhancing your emotional intelligence:

– Practice self-awareness: Self-awareness is the foundation of emotional intelligence. By taking the time to understand your emotions and reactions, you can gain insight into your thoughts, behaviors, and motivations.

– Develop empathy: Empathy is the ability to understand and share the feelings of others. By developing empathy, you can improve your relationships and connect with others on a deeper level.

07: ENHANCING YOUR EMOTIONAL INTELLIGENCE: CONNECTING WITH OTHERS AND YOURSELF

– Manage your emotions: Emotional intelligence requires the ability to manage your emotions in a healthy and productive manner. This means recognizing when you are feeling overwhelmed, taking steps to regulate your emotions, and seeking support when needed.

– Communicate effectively: Effective communication is a key aspect of emotional intelligence. By improving your communication skills, you can build stronger relationships, express your needs and opinions, and resolve conflicts in a positive manner.

– Build strong relationships: Relationships play a critical role in emotional intelligence. By building strong and supportive relationships, you can tap into the emotional support and guidance of others and enhance your emotional intelligence.

– Seek feedback: Feedback can help you improve your emotional intelligence by providing you with insights into your behavior and interactions with others. Seek feedback from trusted individuals, such as friends, family members, or a therapist, to gain a better understanding of your emotional intelligence and areas for improvement.

07: ENHANCING YOUR EMOTIONAL INTELLIGENCE: CONNECTING WITH OTHERS AND YOURSELF

– Engage in personal growth activities: Personal growth activities, such as therapy, self-reflection, and journaling, can help you enhance your emotional intelligence. By exploring your thoughts, feelings, and behaviors, you can gain insight into your emotional intelligence and take steps to improve.

Emotional intelligence is a critical component of success and personal growth. By enhancing your emotional intelligence, you can improve your relationships, boost your self-awareness, and become more resilient in the face of challenges. By incorporating these strategies into your life, you can unleash your potential and transform your life with the proven strategies and techniques for achieving success.

08: Time Management: Maximizing Your Productivity and Efficiency

Time is a valuable resource, and effective time management is essential for success and personal growth. By managing your time effectively, you can maximize your productivity, achieve your goals, and lead a fulfilling life.

Here are some strategies for effective time management:

– Set clear priorities: To effectively manage your time, it is important to have clear priorities. Take the time to identify the most important tasks and activities in your life, and focus your efforts on these.

– Create a schedule: Creating a schedule helps you plan your day, prioritize tasks, and ensure that you are using your time effectively. Use a planner, or schedule your day using a digital tool, such as a calendar app.

– Minimize distractions: Distractions can be a major time-waster, so it is important to minimize them as much as possible. Turn off notifications on your phone, close your email or social media apps when you need to focus, and eliminate

08: TIME MANAGEMENT: MAXIMIZING YOUR PRO-
DUCTIVITY AND EFFICIENCY

other sources of distraction in your environment.

– Learn to say "no": Learning to say "no" is an important part of effective time management. By saying "no" to commitments and activities that are not a priority, you can free up time to focus on what is most important to you.

– Delegate tasks: Delegating tasks to others can help you free up time and reduce your workload. Consider delegating tasks to coworkers, friends, or family members, or consider hiring a virtual assistant to help with administrative tasks.

– Take breaks: Taking regular breaks is important for your health, well-being, and productivity. Take breaks throughout the day to stretch, move, or meditate, to help recharge your batteries and stay focused.

– Evaluate your progress: Regularly evaluate your progress to ensure that you are using your time effectively. Ask yourself if you are making progress towards your goals, and make changes as needed to optimize your time management strategy.

Effective time management is a critical component of success and personal growth. By incorporating these strategies into your life, you can maximize your productivity, achieve your goals, and lead a fulfilling life. By unleashing your potential and transforming your life with the proven strategies and techniques for achieving success, you can achieve success and reach your full potential.

09: Developing a Growth Mindset: Embracing Challenges and Learning from Failure

Your mindset plays a critical role in determining your success and personal growth. By developing a growth mindset, you can embrace challenges, learn from failure, and achieve your goals.

Here are some strategies for developing a growth mindset:

– Embrace challenges: A growth mindset involves embracing challenges and viewing them as opportunities for growth and development. Rather than avoiding challenges or getting discouraged by them, approach them with a positive attitude and a commitment to learning and growth.

– Learn from failure: Failure is an inevitable part of the journey to success. By adopting a growth mindset, you can learn from your failures, using them as opportunities to grow and improve. Reframe your failures as opportunities for growth, and focus on what you can learn from the experience.

– Cultivate a love for learning: A growth mindset involves a love for learning and a commitment to continuous improvement. Make learning a priority in your life, seeking out new experiences and opportunities for growth and development.

– Surround yourself with positive influences: Surrounding yourself with positive influences can help you develop a growth mindset. Seek out individuals who embrace challenges, view failure as an opportunity for growth, and are committed to personal growth and development.

– Reframe negative thoughts: Reframing negative thoughts is an important part of developing a growth mindset. Challenge negative thoughts and beliefs, and replace them with positive, growth-oriented thoughts and beliefs.

– Focus on progress, not perfection: A growth mindset involves a focus on progress, not perfection. Instead of striving for perfection, focus on making progress towards your goals, and celebrating your achievements along the way.

– Embrace change: Embracing change is a key component of a growth mindset. Recognize that change is a natural part of life, and view it as an opportunity for growth and development, rather than as a threat.

09: DEVELOPING A GROWTH MINDSET: EMBRACING CHALLENGES AND LEARNING FROM FAILURE

Developing a growth mindset is a critical component of success and personal growth. By embracing challenges, learning from failure, and cultivating a love for learning, you can unleash your potential and transform your life with the proven strategies and techniques for achieving success. With the ultimate guide to personal growth and fulfillment, you can reach your full potential and achieve the success that you desire.

10: Staying Motivated: Maintaining Focus and Drive

Staying motivated can often be a challenge, especially when we are faced with obstacles and setbacks on our path to success. But the key to overcoming these challenges and maintaining our focus and drive is to have a strong and resilient motivation. In this chapter, we will explore the different strategies and techniques for staying motivated, including setting clear and achievable goals, creating a positive and supportive environment, and developing healthy habits and routines that support our growth and success.

One of the most effective ways to stay motivated is to set clear and achievable goals. This involves breaking down our larger goals into smaller, more manageable steps, and then tracking our progress and celebrating our accomplishments along the way. Setting achievable goals gives us a sense of purpose and direction, and helps us to focus on what we want to achieve and how we can get there.

Another important aspect of staying motivated is creating a positive and supportive environment. This means surrounding ourselves with people who believe in us, support us, and help us to stay focused and motivated. It also means avoiding negative people, situations, and environments that can drain our energy and motivation. By creating a positive and supportive environment, we can feel more confident, inspired, and motivated to pursue our goals.

In addition to setting goals and creating a positive environment, developing healthy habits and routines can also help us to stay motivated. This includes developing healthy sleep patterns, eating well, and engaging in regular physical activity, which can help us to feel more energized, focused, and motivated. It also includes developing positive coping strategies and stress management techniques, which can help us to manage our stress and anxiety levels, and maintain a positive and motivated state of mind.

In conclusion, staying motivated is a critical aspect of achieving success, and requires a combination of clear goals, a positive environment, and healthy habits and routines. By developing these habits and strategies, we can unlock our potential, transform our lives, and achieve the success we desire. So if you want to unleash your potential, stay motivated, and transform your life, remember to focus on your goals, create a positive and supportive environment, and develop healthy habits and routines that support your growth and success.

11: Building Strong Relationships: Connecting with Others and Building a Support System

Building strong relationships is a critical component of personal growth and success. Our social connections play a major role in our happiness and well-being, and can also provide us with the support and encouragement we need to pursue our goals and achieve success. In this chapter, we will explore the importance of building strong relationships, and provide you with tips and strategies for connecting with others and building a supportive network of friends, family, and colleagues.

One of the first steps in building strong relationships is to cultivate a positive and approachable demeanor. People are naturally drawn to individuals who are friendly, open, and authentic, and you can improve your chances of making lasting connections by focusing on your body language, tone of voice, and other nonverbal cues. Additionally, it is important to be a good listener, and to show genuine interest in others and their lives.

Another key aspect of building strong relationships is to be supportive and helpful when others are in need. This might involve lending a listening ear, offering advice, or simply being there for someone when they need a friend. You can also help others by volunteering your time and resources, or by lending your expertise to help others achieve their goals.

In addition to building strong relationships with others, it is also important to cultivate strong relationships with yourself. This involves taking the time to get to know yourself, and to develop a deeper understanding of your values, beliefs, and aspirations. By doing so, you can better understand your own needs and desires, and can work to build relationships that are meaningful and fulfilling.

To help you build strong relationships, it is also important to maintain an open and positive attitude, and to be willing to put in the effort and time required to build meaningful connections. Whether you are seeking to connect with others in your personal life or in your professional life, you can achieve success by focusing on your relationships, and by working to create positive and supportive networks of friends, family, and colleagues.

In conclusion, building strong relationships is a critical

component of personal growth and success. Whether you are looking to build a network of supportive friends and family members, or to connect with others in your professional life, the strategies and techniques outlined in this chapter can help you achieve your goals and unleash your full potential. So why not get started today and start building the strong, supportive relationships that will help you achieve success and fulfillment in all areas of your life!

12: Developing Good Habits: Creating a Blueprint for Success

Habits are routines or patterns of behavior that we engage in regularly without much thought. They are often formed as a result of repeated actions and can have a profound impact on our lives, both positively and negatively. Good habits can help us to achieve our goals and live a successful life, while bad habits can hold us back and prevent us from reaching our full potential.

The Importance of Good Habits

Good habits are the building blocks of success. They help us to create a strong foundation for our lives and provide us with the structure and discipline we need to achieve our goals. They allow us to take control of our lives and make positive changes that can have a lasting impact.

Some of the benefits of good habits include:

– Increased productivity and efficiency

– Improved self-discipline and self-control

– A healthier and happier life

12: DEVELOPING GOOD HABITS: CREATING A BLUE-PRINT FOR SUCCESS

– Increased self-confidence and self-esteem

– A greater sense of purpose and meaning

How to Develop Good Habits

Developing good habits takes time and effort, but it is a worthwhile investment in your future. The following are some tips for developing good habits:

– Start small: It is important to start with small, manageable habits that are easy to integrate into your daily routine. This will help you to establish a sense of momentum and create a foundation for future success.

– Make a plan: Write down your goal and the steps you need to take to achieve it. This will help you to stay focused and motivated.

– Track your progress: Keeping track of your progress can help you to see how far you have come and provide you with a sense of accomplishment.

– Be consistent: Consistency is key when it comes to developing good habits. Try to engage in your desired behavior every day until it becomes automatic.

– Surround yourself with positive influences: Surrounding yourself with positive influences can help you to stay motivated and inspired. Seek out friends, family members, and mentors who support your goals and encourage you to reach your full potential.

Conclusion

Developing good habits is a critical aspect of achieving success. They provide us with the structure and discipline we need to reach our goals and live a fulfilling life. By taking control of our habits and making positive changes, we can unleash our potential and transform our lives. Remember to start small, make a plan, track your progress, be consistent, and surround yourself with positive influences to help you reach your full potential.

13: Effective Communication: Mastering the Art of Conversation

Effective communication is a crucial aspect of personal and professional success. It enables you to build strong relationships, convey your ideas and thoughts effectively, and make meaningful connections with others. In this chapter, we will explore the importance of effective communication and the key skills and techniques you need to master to become a confident and successful communicator.

To begin with, it's essential to understand that effective communication goes beyond just speaking. It encompasses your body language, tone of voice, and the words you choose to use. Communication is a two-way process, and it involves actively listening to others, as well as expressing yourself.

One of the keys to effective communication is being able to communicate clearly and concisely. This means avoiding filler words, using simple language, and getting to the point. It's also important to be mindful of your tone of voice and body language, as these can have a significant impact on how your message is received.

Another important aspect of effective communication is active listening. This means giving your full attention to the person speaking, making eye contact, and avoiding distractions. It's essential to understand that effective communication is not just about expressing yourself, but also about understanding and interpreting the messages of others.

In addition to active listening, it's also crucial to develop your empathy skills. Empathy involves putting yourself in the other person's shoes and understanding their perspective. This can help to build trust and rapport, and it's essential in resolving conflicts and building strong relationships.

When it comes to expressing yourself, it's essential to be confident and assertive. This means standing up for your beliefs and opinions while being respectful of others. It's important to remember that effective communication is not about winning arguments or getting your own way, but rather about finding common ground and building understanding.

Another important aspect of effective communication is nonverbal communication. This includes your body language, facial expressions, and gestures. Nonverbal communication can often convey a message more effectively than words, and it's essential to be mindful of the signals you are sending through your nonverbal cues.

In conclusion, effective communication is a vital skill that can help you to achieve success in all areas of your life. Whether it's in your personal relationships or in the work-place, the ability to communicate effectively can open up new opportunities and enhance your overall quality of life. By mastering the key skills and techniques outlined in this chapter, you can unleash your potential and transform your life through the power of effective communication.

14: Networking: Building Professional Relationships

Networking is a critical aspect of success, especially in a professional setting. Building strong and meaningful relationships with others can help you open doors, gain new opportunities, and advance your career. In this chapter, we will explore the key principles of effective networking and provide you with the tools you need to build meaningful relationships with others.

The first step to successful networking is to have a clear understanding of your goals. Are you looking to expand your professional circle, meet potential collaborators, or simply make new friends? Having a clear goal in mind will help you focus your efforts and prioritize your activities.

Next, it is important to put yourself in situations where you can meet new people. Attend networking events, join professional organizations, and take advantage of opportunities to engage with others in your field. You can also expand your network by reaching out to people you admire and respect, or by taking advantage of social media platforms like LinkedIn, Twitter, and Facebook.

14: NETWORKING: BUILDING PROFESSIONAL RELATIONSHIPS

When networking, it is important to be yourself and to make a genuine connection with others. Be friendly and approachable, and be willing to listen and engage in conversation. Avoid being overly pushy or self-promoting, as this can turn people off and undermine your efforts to build strong relationships.

Another key aspect of effective networking is to add value to the lives of others. This could involve offering helpful advice, sharing your knowledge and experience, or making introductions to others in your network. By providing value to others, you will be more likely to build strong relationships and establish a positive reputation.

Finally, it is important to follow up with the people you meet and maintain your relationships over time. This could involve reaching out to connect on social media, sending a quick email to say hello, or inviting someone to lunch or coffee. By taking the time to nurture your relationships, you will deepen your connections and build a strong network of support.

In conclusion, networking is a powerful tool for success and can help you achieve your goals, expand your opportunities,

and build meaningful relationships with others. By following the principles outlined in this chapter, you can develop a
strong network of support and unlock your full potential for
success.

15: Financial Management: Creating and Maintaining Wealth

Financial management is an essential aspect of success and a critical factor in achieving your goals. Whether you're working towards financial independence, saving for retirement, or just trying to live within your means, it's crucial to understand the principles of financial management and how to effectively manage your finances.

The first step in financial management is setting a budget. A budget helps you understand your current financial situation and keeps you on track as you work towards your financial goals. When creating a budget, it's important to consider all of your income sources and all of your expenses, including fixed expenses such as rent or mortgage payments and variable expenses like groceries and entertainment.

Next, it's essential to prioritize your spending. This means deciding which expenses are most important to you and allocating your budget accordingly. For example, you may choose to allocate a higher percentage of your budget to saving for retirement or paying off debt, while cutting back on discretionary spending like dining out or entertainment.

15: FINANCIAL MANAGEMENT: CREATING AND MAIN-TAINING WEALTH

In addition to budgeting and prioritizing spending, it's important to have a plan for managing debt. This may include paying off high-interest credit card debt, consolidating debt, or negotiating lower interest rates with your creditors. Having a debt management plan in place will help you pay off debt faster and improve your credit score.

Investing is another important aspect of financial management. Whether you're just starting out or you're looking to grow your wealth, it's essential to understand the basics of investing and how to create a diversified portfolio. This may include stocks, bonds, real estate, and other investments.

Finally, it's crucial to have an emergency fund. This is a savings account specifically set aside for unexpected expenses, like a car repair or a medical emergency. Having an emergency fund can provide peace of mind and help you avoid going into debt when faced with unexpected expenses.

In conclusion, financial management is an essential aspect of success and a critical factor in achieving your goals. By setting a budget, prioritizing spending, managing debt, investing, and having an emergency fund, you can create and maintain wealth, and achieve financial independence. Remember, success in any area of your life requires discipline, dedication, and a commitment to personal growth and self-improvement.

16: Mindfulness and Meditation: Finding Inner Peace and Balance

Mindfulness and meditation are powerful tools that can help you achieve success in all areas of your life. By incorporating these practices into your daily routine, you can increase your focus and concentration, reduce stress and anxiety, and cultivate a more positive outlook. In this chapter, we will explore the many benefits of mindfulness and meditation, and how you can incorporate these practices into your life to unlock your full potential and transform your life.

The concept of mindfulness can be traced back thousands of years to the teachings of Eastern philosophers and spiritual leaders. Mindfulness involves paying attention to the present moment, without judgment or distraction. This can be achieved through meditation, mindfulness exercises, and simply paying attention to the sensations and thoughts that arise in the moment.

One of the main benefits of mindfulness is that it helps you become more aware of your thoughts and emotions, allowing you to gain control over them, rather than letting them control you. When you are more aware of your thoughts and emotions, you can respond to them in a more positive and productive way, leading to greater success and satisfaction in all areas of your life.

Meditation is another powerful tool for personal growth and transformation. It is a method of quieting the mind and focusing on the present moment. Through regular meditation, you can develop greater self-awareness, increase your ability to focus and concentrate, and reduce stress and anxiety. In addition, meditation has been shown to improve physical health by reducing blood pressure and improving sleep patterns.

Incorporating mindfulness and meditation into your daily routine can be simple and easy. Start by setting aside a few minutes each day to simply sit quietly and focus on your breath. As you become more comfortable with these practices, you can increase the amount of time you spend meditating, or try more advanced techniques such as guided meditations or mindfulness exercises.

In conclusion, mindfulness and meditation are powerful tools for personal growth and transformation, helping you achieve success in all areas of your life. By incorporating these practices into your daily routine, you can increase your focus and concentration, reduce stress and anxiety, and cultivate a more positive outlook, leading to greater success and satisfaction in all areas of your life.

17: Physical Well-Being: Taking Care of Your Body and Mind

The pursuit of success often requires a great deal of focus and energy, but it is essential to remember that our bodies and minds are interconnected, and neglecting either one can negatively impact our overall wellbeing and ability to achieve our goals. In this chapter, we will explore the importance of physical well-being and the various ways in which it can support our journey towards success.

One of the most important aspects of physical well-being is maintaining a healthy diet. Our bodies require the right balance of nutrients and vitamins to function at their best, and the food we eat plays a critical role in providing these essential components. A diet that is rich in fruits, vegetables, whole grains, and lean proteins can help boost energy levels, improve mental clarity, and support physical endurance. Additionally, it is important to drink plenty of water and limit our consumption of sugary and fatty foods, as these can lead to weight gain, decreased energy, and a variety of health problems.

In addition to maintaining a healthy diet, it is also crucial to engage in regular physical activity. Exercise is an essential component of physical well-being, as it helps to keep our bodies strong and healthy, improves cardiovascular health, and reduces the risk of chronic diseases such as heart disease, diabetes, and cancer. Regular physical activity can also help to boost mood, reduce stress, and improve sleep quality, all of which are critical for maintaining good physical and mental health.

Other important aspects of physical well-being include getting enough sleep, managing stress levels, and avoiding harmful substances such as tobacco and excessive alcohol consumption. Sleep is essential for physical and mental recovery, and not getting enough sleep can lead to decreased energy levels, decreased cognitive function, and an increased risk of health problems. Stress can also have a significant impact on our physical and mental health, and it is essential to find healthy ways to manage stress, such as through exercise, mindfulness practices, and stress-management techniques.

Finally, it is important to seek regular medical check-ups and preventive care to maintain good physical health. Regular check-ups can help to detect and treat potential health problems before they become more serious, and preventive care can help to maintain good health and reduce the risk of chronic diseases.

In conclusion, physical well-being is a critical component of success and should not be overlooked. By maintaining a healthy diet, engaging in regular physical activity, getting enough sleep, managing stress, avoiding harmful substances, and seeking regular medical care, we can support our bodies and minds on our journey towards success. With a focus on physical well-being, we can unleash our full potential and transform our lives with the proven strategies and techniques for achieving success.

18: Stress Management: Coping with Life's Challenges

Stress is a normal part of life, and everyone experiences it at some point. Whether it's due to work, personal relationships, financial worries, or other life events, stress can take a toll on our mental and physical well-being. The good news is that there are many strategies and techniques that can help you manage stress and cope with life's challenges more effectively. In this chapter, we'll explore some of the most effective methods for managing stress and achieving greater balance and peace of mind.

Understand the Sources of Stress

The first step in managing stress is to understand its sources. This can be difficult, as stress can come from many different sources, including work, finances, relationships, health problems, and more. However, by taking some time to reflect on the sources of stress in your life, you can begin to develop a better understanding of what's causing your stress and what you can do to manage it.

For example, you may find that your job is a major source of stress. If this is the case, you may need to consider finding a new job, or taking steps to reduce stress at your current job. On the other hand, you may find that financial worries are the root of your stress. If this is the case, you may need to create a budget, reduce your expenses, or seek help from a financial advisor.

Identify Your Stress Triggers

Once you understand the sources of stress in your life, it's important to identify your stress triggers. Stress triggers are the specific events, situations, or circumstances that cause you to feel stressed. By identifying your stress triggers, you can take steps to avoid or minimize your exposure to them.

For example, you may find that traffic jams are a major stress trigger for you. If this is the case, you may need to find a different route to work or take public transportation. Alternatively, you may find that public speaking is a major stress trigger for you. If this is the case, you may need to take steps to build your confidence and improve your public speaking skills.

Practice Relaxation Techniques

Relaxation techniques can be very effective for reducing stress and promoting a sense of well-being. Some of the most popular and effective relaxation techniques include deep breathing, progressive muscle relaxation, guided imagery, and yoga.

Deep breathing involves taking slow, deep breaths and focusing on the sensation of air entering and leaving your body. Progressive muscle relaxation involves tensing and relaxing different muscle groups to reduce physical tension and promote relaxation. Guided imagery involves using your imagination to visualize a peaceful, calming scene, and can be very effective for reducing stress and promoting a sense of calm. Yoga is a physical and mental practice that involves stretching, strengthening, and focusing the mind, and can be a great way to reduce stress and promote well-being.

Develop a Support System

Having a strong support system is an important part of managing stress and coping with life's challenges. Whether it's friends, family members, co-workers, or a mental health professional, having people you can turn to for support and encouragement can make a big difference in your ability to manage stress and maintain a positive outlook.

If you don't already have a strong support system, it may be helpful to seek out new relationships and connections. You can do this by joining a club or organization, volunteering, or simply reaching out to people you admire and respect.

Take Care of Your Physical Health

Taking care of your physical health is an important part of managing stress and promoting overall well-being. This includes eating a healthy diet, getting enough sleep, and engaging in regular physical activity.

19: Self-Care: Putting Yourself First and Taking Time for Yourself

Self-care is an often overlooked aspect of personal growth and success. Many people believe that success requires sacrifice and putting oneself last, but this simply is not true. To achieve true success, one must prioritize their own well-being and engage in self-care practices that nourish both their mind and body. In this chapter, we will explore the importance of self-care and provide tips and techniques for incorporating it into your daily routine.

Why is Self-Care Important?

Self-care is essential for both our physical and mental health. When we neglect our own needs, our bodies and minds suffer, and our ability to perform at our best is diminished. Neglecting self-care can lead to physical and mental burnout, depression, anxiety, and a host of other health problems.

By prioritizing self-care, we ensure that we have the energy and resources necessary to tackle the challenges of daily life and achieve our goals. Self-care helps us maintain a positive outlook, boosts our confidence, and improves our overall well-being.

Types of Self-Care

There are many different types of self-care, including physical self-care, emotional self-care, mental self-care, and spiritual self-care. Physical self-care involves taking care of our bodies through exercise, proper nutrition, and getting adequate rest. Emotional self-care involves taking time to process and manage our emotions, and engaging in activities that bring us joy and fulfillment. Mental self-care involves engaging in activities that stimulate our minds, such as reading, learning, or problem-solving. Spiritual self-care involves connecting with a higher power or finding meaning and purpose in life.

Incorporating Self-Care into Your Daily Routine

Self-care can seem like a daunting task, especially for those who are already stretched thin. However, incorporating self-care into your daily routine does not have to be difficult or time-consuming. Here are some tips for making self-care a priority in your life:

19: SELF-CARE: PUTTING YOURSELF FIRST AND TAKING TIME FOR YOURSELF

– Make time for self-care. Set aside time each day for self-care, even if it's just a few minutes. This can be as simple as taking a walk, reading a book, or practicing mindfulness.

– Prioritize self-care activities that you enjoy. Choose self-care activities that bring you joy and fulfillment. This will help you look forward to your self-care time and make it a more enjoyable experience.

– Practice self-care in small ways. Small acts of self-care can have a big impact on our well-being. Take a relaxing bath, meditate, or treat yourself to a healthy snack.

– Find a self-care buddy. Consider partnering with a friend or family member to hold each other accountable and encourage one another to prioritize self-care.

– Make self-care a non-negotiable. Just as you would prioritize other important aspects of your life, make self-care a non-negotiable. Put it on your calendar, and treat it with the same importance as other appointments.

In conclusion, self-care is an essential aspect of personal growth and success. By incorporating self-care into your daily routine, you can improve your physical and mental health, boost your confidence, and maintain a positive outlook. Remember, taking care of yourself should always be a top priority. By putting yourself first, you are setting yourself up for success in all areas of your life.

20: Entrepreneurship: Starting and Growing Your Own Business

Entrepreneurship is one of the most fulfilling and challenging paths to success. As an entrepreneur, you have the opportunity to create something from scratch, build a business that you're passionate about, and make a positive impact on the world. However, starting and growing a business is also a long and difficult journey that requires hard work, dedication, and the ability to persevere through failures and setbacks.

In this chapter, we will explore the fundamentals of entrepreneurship and provide you with proven strategies and techniques for starting and growing your own business. Whether you're just starting out or you're looking to take your existing business to the next level, this guide will help you achieve success as an entrepreneur.

The first step in starting a business is to identify your area of expertise. What are you passionate about? What are you good at? What problem can you solve? These are all important questions that will help you determine what type of business you should start.

20: ENTREPRENEURSHIP: STARTING AND GROWING YOUR OWN BUSINESS

Once you have an idea of what you want to do, it's time to validate your idea. This means researching your market to determine if there is a demand for your product or service. You can use tools like surveys, market research, and competitive analysis to help you make this determination.

Once you have validated your idea, it's time to create a business plan. This plan should include your business goals, target market, marketing strategy, financial projections, and more. Your business plan will serve as your roadmap for success and will help you stay on track as you work to build your business.

Next, you'll need to secure funding for your business. There are a number of ways to do this, including taking out a loan, getting investment from friends and family, or seeking venture capital. It's important to have a solid understanding of your financial needs before you start your business and to have a clear plan for how you'll use your funds to grow your business.

Once you have funding in place, it's time to start building your business. This involves hiring employees, setting up your infrastructure, and working on your marketing and sales strategy. As your business grows, it's important to stay focused on your goals and to continuously work to improve your processes and systems.

Growing your business is a never-ending process, but there are a number of proven strategies that can help you succeed. One of the most important things you can do is to continually innovate and bring new products and services to market. You should also focus on building strong relationships with your customers and partners, and on maintaining a positive and supportive company culture.

Another key to success as an entrepreneur is to continually work on your personal growth. This means developing new skills, seeking out new opportunities, and surrounding yourself with positive, supportive people. The more you grow as a person, the more you will be able to grow your business.

In conclusion, starting and growing a business is a long and difficult journey, but it is also one of the most rewarding paths to success. By following the strategies and techniques outlined in this chapter, you can unleash your entrepreneurial potential and transform your life. With hard work, dedication, and a positive mental attitude, you can achieve your goals and build a successful and fulfilling business.

21: Leadership: Inspiring and Guiding Others to Success

Leadership is a critical component of success, and it is the ability to inspire and guide others towards a common goal. It is the foundation for creating a successful team and achieving great things. A great leader can bring out the best in others, and they can motivate, encourage, and direct their team towards success.

To be an effective leader, it is important to understand the characteristics that define great leaders. Some of the key traits of great leaders include integrity, honesty, confidence, empathy, vision, and the ability to inspire and motivate others. In addition, a great leader must be able to communicate effectively, establish trust, and create a sense of belonging among their team.

Another important aspect of leadership is setting an example. As a leader, it is your responsibility to lead by example, and this includes demonstrating the values and behavior that you expect from others. For example, if you value honesty and transparency, you must demonstrate these qualities in your own behavior.

21: LEADERSHIP: INSPIRING AND GUIDING OTHERS TO SUCCESS

Leadership also requires the ability to make decisions. A great leader must be able to make difficult decisions, and they must be willing to take responsibility for the outcome. This requires a level of courage and the ability to think critically and act strategically.

In addition to the qualities listed above, great leaders must also be able to inspire and motivate others. Inspiration comes from within, and it is the ability to see the potential in others and help them realize their own potential. Motivation, on the other hand, comes from without, and it is the drive that comes from a clear understanding of what is expected and what is possible.

To be an effective leader, it is also important to be a good communicator. Communication is the key to establishing trust and building relationships, and it is critical for inspiring and guiding others towards success. A great leader must be able to articulate their vision, listen to feedback, and be open and transparent in their communication.

Leadership also requires the ability to develop and maintain a supportive team. This means that a great leader must be able to create an environment where team members feel valued, supported, and encouraged. This requires the ability to understand the strengths and weaknesses of each team member, and to provide support and guidance where it is needed.

Finally, leadership requires a long-term commitment to personal growth and development. A great leader must be committed to their own personal growth, and they must be willing to invest the time and effort necessary to improve their skills and knowledge. This requires the ability to reflect on their own behavior and make changes where necessary, and it also requires a commitment to continuous learning and improvement.

In conclusion, leadership is a critical component of success, and it is the ability to inspire and guide others towards a common goal. It requires a combination of qualities, including integrity, confidence, empathy, and the ability to communicate effectively and make decisions. A great leader must also be committed to their own personal growth, and they must be willing to invest the time and effort necessary to improve their skills and knowledge. By embracing these qualities, and by striving for continuous improvement, you can become a great leader and inspire others to achieve suc-

cess.

22: Innovation: Embracing Change and Thinking Outside the Box

Innovation is a crucial aspect of success, and it's what sets successful individuals and organizations apart from the rest. It's about being creative, thinking outside the box, and embracing change. This chapter will explore the importance of innovation and provide you with the tools and techniques you need to foster an innovative mindset and approach to life.

First and foremost, it's important to understand that innovation is not just about coming up with new ideas and inventions. It's also about the ability to apply existing ideas in new and creative ways, to challenge the status quo and push the boundaries of what's possible.

To become more innovative, it's important to cultivate a growth mindset. This means embracing challenges and being willing to take risks, even if they lead to failure. It's also important to seek out new experiences and opportunities to learn, as this can help you develop a more diverse skill set and expose you to new perspectives and ideas.

67

22: INNOVATION: EMBRACING CHANGE AND THINKING OUTSIDE THE BOX

In addition to fostering a growth mindset, it's also important to cultivate a supportive environment that encourages innovation. This means surrounding yourself with people who are creative and open-minded, and creating a workplace culture that values innovation and rewards creative thinking.

To further develop your innovation skills, consider taking courses or attending workshops that focus on creativity and innovation. You can also engage in activities like brainstorming sessions, design thinking exercises, and rapid prototyping to help you develop your problem-solving skills and get into the habit of thinking creatively.

It's also important to stay informed about the latest trends and developments in your field, as this can give you ideas for new products, services, and technologies that you can develop or improve upon. And don't be afraid to ask questions and seek out feedback from others, as this can help you gain new insights and perspectives that can lead to innovation.

Ultimately, innovation is about constantly striving to improve, to find new and better ways of doing things, and to make a positive impact on the world. By embracing a growth mindset, fostering a supportive environment, and engaging in activities that foster innovation, you can unleash your potential and transform your life.

In conclusion, innovation is a crucial aspect of success, and it's what sets successful individuals and organizations apart from the rest. By cultivating a growth mindset, fostering a supportive environment, and engaging in activities that foster innovation, you can unleash your potential and transform your life. With the right tools and techniques, anyone can develop the skills they need to become more innovative, and to make a positive impact on the world.

23: Decision Making: Navigating Life's Choices with Confidence

Making decisions is a daily part of life, and being able to make good ones is critical to our success. Whether it's a small decision like what to eat for lunch or a larger one like which job to take, each decision we make has the potential to shape our lives and influence our future. Unfortunately, many of us struggle with making decisions, often feeling overwhelmed and unsure of what to do. This can lead to indecision, missed opportunities, and even regret.

The good news is that decision-making is a skill that can be developed and improved with practice. By understanding the decision-making process and learning some key strategies, you can become a confident and effective decision-maker, capable of navigating life's choices with ease. In this chapter, we will explore the decision-making process, identify common obstacles to effective decision-making, and provide you with practical tools and techniques to help you make better decisions.

The Decision-Making Process

The decision-making process begins with identifying the

problem or opportunity at hand. Once you have a clear understanding of the situation, it's time to gather information and consider your options. This is where you will do research, ask for advice, and evaluate the pros and cons of each option. After weighing your options, it's time to make a decision and take action. Finally, it's important to reflect on the decision you made and learn from the outcome. This feedback loop will help you improve your decision-making skills over time.

Overcoming Common Obstacles

One of the biggest obstacles to effective decision-making is fear. Fear of making the wrong decision, fear of failure, and fear of the unknown can all prevent us from making decisions with confidence. To overcome this obstacle, it's important to acknowledge your fears and understand that making mistakes is a natural part of the decision-making process. You can also practice mindfulness techniques to help reduce anxiety and stay focused on the present moment.

Another common obstacle to effective decision-making is cognitive biases. These biases are unconscious tendencies that can distort our perception and impact our decision-making ability. Some of the most common cognitive biases include confirmation bias, sunk cost fallacy, and framing effects. To overcome these biases, it's important to be aware of them and to actively work to counteract them.

Tools and Techniques for Better Decision-Making

There are many tools and techniques that can help you make better decisions. Here are a few of the most effective:

– The Pros and Cons List: This is a simple and effective tool for weighing your options and considering the potential outcomes of each decision. Simply write down the pros and cons of each option and compare them to determine the best course of action.

– The Cost-Benefit Analysis: This is a more formal and structured method of evaluating the potential outcomes of a decision. You will calculate the costs and benefits of each option and use this information to make a decision.

– The Pareto Principle: This principle states that 80% of your results will come from 20% of your efforts. When making a decision, focus on the options that will have the greatest impact and prioritize those over others.

– The 80/20 Rule: Similar to the Pareto Principle, the 80/20 rule states that 80% of your results come from 20% of your actions. When making a decision, focus on the actions that will have the greatest impact and prioritize those over others.

– The SWOT Analysis: This tool is used to evaluate the strengths, weaknesses, opportunities, and threats of a decision. By understanding these factors, you can make a more informed and confident decision.

24: Creative Problem Solving: Overcoming Obstacles with Innovation

In life, we are constantly faced with challenges and obstacles that can test our resolve and hinder our progress towards success. However, what separates successful people from the rest is their ability to find creative and innovative solutions to these challenges. In this chapter, we will explore the art of creative problem solving and how you can develop this skill to overcome the obstacles in your life and achieve greater success.

What is Creative Problem Solving?

Creative problem solving is the process of using imagination and original ideas to find solutions to complex problems. It involves breaking down problems into smaller, manageable parts, and exploring multiple possibilities before arriving at a solution. Unlike traditional problem solving, which focuses on finding the most obvious or practical solution, creative problem solving allows you to think outside the box and come up with innovative and unconventional solutions.

Why is Creative Problem Solving Important for Success?

24: CREATIVE PROBLEM SOLVING: OVERCOMING OBSTACLES WITH INNOVATION

In today's fast-paced and rapidly changing world, the ability to think creatively and find innovative solutions to problems has never been more important. Successful people are able to overcome challenges and find creative solutions to problems, which allows them to achieve their goals and move forward towards their dreams.

In addition, creative problem solving helps you to develop a growth mindset and embrace challenges as opportunities for growth and development. It also helps you to build resilience, as you learn to overcome obstacles and find new and innovative ways to achieve your goals.

How to Develop Your Creative Problem Solving Skills

There are several strategies and techniques you can use to develop your creative problem solving skills, including:

– Start with a positive attitude: A positive attitude is key to creative problem solving. When you approach a problem with a positive and optimistic outlook, you are more likely to find innovative solutions.

– Get organized: Make sure to have a clear understanding of

the problem you are trying to solve. Break down the problem into smaller parts and create a plan of action.

– Brainstorm: One of the most effective ways to develop creative solutions is to brainstorm with others. Gather a group of people who have different perspectives and experiences, and encourage open and honest discussion.

– Keep an open mind: Be open to new ideas and perspectives, and don't be afraid to try new things. You never know when an unconventional solution will lead to the greatest success.

– Experiment: Experiment with different approaches and solutions until you find the one that works best for you. Don't be afraid to make mistakes, as this is often where the greatest learning opportunities lie.

– Reframe the problem: Instead of looking at a problem as a roadblock, try to reframe it as an opportunity for growth and development. By looking at challenges in a new light, you may be able to find creative solutions that you wouldn't have considered otherwise.

24: CREATIVE PROBLEM SOLVING: OVERCOMING OBSTACLES WITH INNOVATION

– Take breaks: When you're stuck on a problem, take a break and do something that you enjoy. This will help you to clear your mind and come back to the problem with fresh ideas.

– Stay persistent: Finally, it's important to stay persistent and not give up on finding a solution. With determination and perseverance, you can overcome any obstacle and achieve your goals.

Conclusion

Creative problem solving is a valuable skill that can help you overcome obstacles and achieve greater success in life. By developing your ability to think outside the box and find innovative solutions, you will be able to face challenges with confidence and resilience. So start using these techniques today, and unleash your potential for success.

25: Personal Development: Continuously Improving Yourself

Personal development is an ongoing journey, and one of the keys to unlocking your full potential and achieving success in all areas of your life. Personal development is about taking responsibility for your own growth, learning new skills and knowledge, and continuously improving yourself in order to reach your goals and live the life you want.

To begin your journey of personal development, it's important to start with a clear understanding of your values and goals. Take some time to reflect on what is truly important to you in life, and what you want to achieve. This could include personal goals such as developing closer relationships, improving your health and well-being, or growing your career. It could also include broader goals such as making a positive impact on the world, or contributing to society in some way.

Once you have a clear understanding of your values and goals, you can start to create a plan for how to achieve them. This may involve setting specific, measurable, achievable, relevant, and time-bound (SMART) goals, breaking down larger goals into smaller, manageable steps, and establishing habits and routines that support your personal develop-ment. For example, if your goal is to improve your health and well-being, you may set a goal to exercise for 30 minutes a day, and to eat a healthy diet.

One of the most important aspects of personal development is continuous learning. This could involve formal education and training, such as taking courses or attending work-shops, or it could involve more informal learning opportun-ities, such as reading books and articles, or listening to pod-casts. It's important to be proactive about seeking out new knowledge and skills that will help you achieve your goals, and to continually challenge yourself to grow and improve.

Along with continuous learning, it's also important to prac-tice self-reflection and introspection. Take the time to regu-larly reflect on your thoughts, emotions, and behaviors, and to understand how they may be impacting your life and your personal development. This could involve journaling, meditating, or talking to a trusted friend or mentor.

Another key aspect of personal development is developing positive habits and behaviors. This could involve creating routines that support your goals, such as waking up early to exercise or going to bed early to ensure a good night's sleep. It could also involve replacing negative behaviors and habits with positive ones, such as replacing unhealthy snacking with healthier options, or replacing negative self-talk with positive affirmations.

Finally, it's important to surround yourself with a supportive network of friends, family, and mentors who can offer encouragement, guidance, and accountability as you work towards your goals. Seek out relationships with people who have similar values and goals, and who will support and challenge you in your journey of personal development.

In conclusion, personal development is an ongoing journey, and one of the keys to unlocking your full potential and achieving success in all areas of your life. By setting clear goals, engaging in continuous learning, practicing self-reflection, developing positive habits and behaviors, and building a supportive network of relationships, you can transform your life and achieve the success you want.

26: Learning and Development: Staying Relevant and Adapting to Change

Successful individuals understand that their personal and professional growth is a continuous journey, and that learning and development are essential components of this journey. In today's rapidly changing world, it is more important than ever to stay current and adapt to new technologies, trends, and ideas. By engaging in regular learning and development activities, you can increase your knowledge, skills, and abilities, and better position yourself for success.

One of the key benefits of learning and development is the ability to stay relevant in your field. With the increasing pace of change, many traditional careers and industries are becoming obsolete, while new ones are emerging. By continuously learning, you can stay current with the latest advancements in your field, and better prepare yourself for new opportunities. This not only increases your employability, but it also keeps you engaged and motivated in your work.

Another important aspect of learning and development is

the ability to adapt to change. The world is constantly evolving, and those who are able to adapt to new circumstances are the ones who are most likely to succeed. By continually learning and growing, you become more flexible and open-minded, allowing you to embrace change and navigate through life's challenges with confidence.

There are many ways to engage in learning and development activities. Some popular options include taking courses, attending workshops and conferences, reading books and articles, and pursuing professional certifications. The key is to find what works best for you, and to make learning and development a regular part of your routine.

In order to be successful, it is also important to have a growth mindset. This means embracing challenges and seeing them as opportunities for growth, rather than as obstacles. By having a growth mindset, you are more likely to seek out new learning experiences and to persevere through difficult situations.

One way to cultivate a growth mindset is by setting goals and tracking your progress. When you set specific, measurable goals for your learning and development, you are more likely to stay focused and motivated. Additionally, tracking your progress can help you see how far you have come, and can provide you with the encouragement you need to keep going.

In conclusion, learning and development are essential components of success, and are critical for staying relevant and adapting to change. Whether you are looking to improve your career prospects, stay current in your field, or simply pursue personal growth, engaging in regular learning and development activities can help you achieve your goals. So embrace the journey, set goals, and never stop learning!

27: Sales and Marketing: Promoting Your Ideas and Products

Sales and marketing are two critical components of success in any business. The ability to effectively promote your ideas and products is essential for attracting customers and building a successful brand. In today's fast-paced and ever-changing market, having a strong sales and marketing strategy is more important than ever. Whether you're starting a new business or trying to grow an existing one, the strategies and techniques outlined in this chapter will help you achieve your goals.

Understanding Your Target Market:

The first step in creating an effective sales and marketing strategy is to understand your target market. This includes identifying your ideal customer, understanding their needs and preferences, and learning what motivates them to make a purchase. By understanding your target market, you can create a marketing campaign that speaks directly to them and resonates with their interests.

Developing a Unique Selling Proposition:

27: SALES AND MARKETING: PROMOTING YOUR IDEAS AND PRODUCTS

A unique selling proposition (USP) is a statement that sets your product or service apart from your competitors. It's what makes your offering unique and desirable to your target market. Your USP should be short, simple, and easy to remember. It should convey the benefits of your product or service in a way that sets you apart from your competition.

Creating a Marketing Plan:

Once you have a clear understanding of your target market and a unique selling proposition, it's time to create a marketing plan. This plan should outline the steps you'll take to reach your target market and promote your product or service. It should include a detailed description of your marketing strategy, your target audience, your marketing budget, and your goals and objectives.

Developing a Strong Online Presence:

In today's digital age, having a strong online presence is essential for any business. Your website should be well-designed, easy to navigate, and optimized for search engines. You should also have a strong social media presence, with a consistent brand message across all platforms. Additionally, you may want to consider investing in online advertising, such as Google AdWords or Facebook Ads, to reach your target market more effectively.

Building Relationships with Your Customers:

Building strong relationships with your customers is critical to success in sales and marketing. This includes providing excellent customer service, responding to customer inquiries in a timely manner, and following up with customers after a sale. By building strong relationships with your customers, you'll create loyal fans who are more likely to recommend your product or service to others.

Closing the Sale:

Closing the sale is the final step in the sales and marketing process. This involves persuading your potential customer to make a purchase. To close the sale, you need to understand their needs, address any objections they may have, and build rapport with them. It's also important to provide a clear and compelling call-to-action, such as asking for the sale or offering a special promotion.

27: SALES AND MARKETING: PROMOTING YOUR IDEAS AND PRODUCTS

Conclusion:

Sales and marketing are essential components of success in any business. By understanding your target market, developing a unique selling proposition, creating a marketing plan, building a strong online presence, building relationships with your customers, and closing the sale, you can effectively promote your ideas and products and achieve your goals. Remember, success in sales and marketing requires persistence, patience, and a willingness to continually learn and adapt to new technologies and trends. With the right strategies and techniques, you can unleash your potential and transform your life by taking control of your financial future.

28: Creativity: Unleashing Your Imagination and Achieving Your Dreams

Creativity is the lifeblood of innovation, progress, and growth. It's a critical component of human existence that helps us make sense of the world around us and bring new ideas, perspectives, and solutions to the table. Without creativity, we'd be stuck in the same patterns of thought and behavior, never advancing or discovering new possibilities. That's why harnessing the power of your imagination and creativity is key to unleashing your potential and transforming your life.

One of the greatest challenges to unlocking your creativity is fear. Fear of the unknown, fear of failure, fear of criticism – all of these can stifle your imagination and keep you from exploring new ideas and avenues. But by overcoming these fears and embracing your creative side, you can open up a world of possibilities and opportunities for yourself.

So, how can you unleash your creativity and start living the life of your dreams? Here are some proven strategies and techniques for achieving success through creativity:

28: CREATIVITY: UNLEASHING YOUR IMAGINATION AND ACHIEVING YOUR DREAMS

– Embrace your uniqueness: Everyone has a unique perspective, set of experiences, and talents. By embracing your individuality and being true to yourself, you can tap into your creative potential and bring new ideas and solutions to the table.

– Cultivate a growth mindset: Creativity is not a fixed trait – it can be developed and grown with practice. By adopting a growth mindset and embracing challenges and failures as opportunities to learn and grow, you can unlock your imagination and reach new heights of creative expression.

– Take breaks: Creativity often flourishes when you step away from your routine and allow yourself time to think and reflect. Whether it's taking a walk in nature, trying a new hobby, or simply taking a nap, taking breaks can help you recharge and come back to your work with fresh perspective and renewed energy.

– Surround yourself with inspiration: The people, places, and things you surround yourself with can have a huge impact on your creativity. Seek out inspiring environments, surround yourself with positive and supportive people, and seek out sources of inspiration, such as art, music, and nature.

– Experiment and take risks: Creativity often stems from trying new things and stepping outside of your comfort zone. By experimenting and taking risks, you can explore new ideas and perspectives and discover new ways of thinking and problem-solving.

– Collaborate with others: Collaborating with others can not only help you gain new perspectives and ideas, but also bring a sense of camaraderie and support to your creative endeavors. Whether it's working with a colleague on a project, participating in a creative writing group, or simply bouncing ideas off of a trusted friend, collaborating can help you grow and expand your creative horizons.

– Reflect and evaluate: Regular reflection and evaluation can help you track your progress and identify areas where you need to grow and improve. By reflecting on your creative endeavors, you can identify areas where you need to push yourself further and gain a deeper understanding of your strengths and weaknesses as a creative individual.

By implementing these strategies and techniques, you can

unleash your imagination and start living the life of your dreams. Remember, creativity is not just about artistic expression – it's a critical component of personal growth and fulfillment that can help you achieve success in all areas of your life. So embrace your individuality, cultivate a growth mindset, surround yourself with inspiration, and never stop exploring, experimenting, and pushing your boundaries. With persistence and dedication, you can achieve anything you set your mind to and unleash your full potential as a creative individual.

29: Branding: Building Your Personal and Professional Reputation

Branding is the process of creating, establishing, and promoting a unique image and identity for yourself, your products, or your services. In today's highly competitive world, building and maintaining a strong personal and professional reputation is essential for success, as it helps you stand out from the crowd and establish trust and credibility with your target audience.

But building a strong brand is not just about creating a logo or tagline – it's about creating a consistent, meaningful, and memorable experience for those who interact with you. Here are some proven strategies and techniques for building your personal and professional reputation and establishing a strong brand:

– Define your values and purpose: A strong brand is built on a foundation of purpose, values, and beliefs. Start by defining what's important to you, what you stand for, and what you want to achieve. This will help you create a clear and consistent message that resonates with your target audience.

— Know your audience: Understanding your target audience is key to building a strong brand. Identify your target market, understand their needs, and tailor your message and branding to their interests and preferences.

— Create a visual identity: Your visual identity is the cornerstone of your brand and includes your logo, website, business cards, and any other visual elements that represent you or your business. Invest in a professional design that accurately represents your brand and sets you apart from the competition.

— Be consistent: Consistency is key to building a strong brand. Make sure that your messaging, visuals, and interactions are consistent across all platforms and touchpoints. This helps create a memorable and recognizable brand that your audience can trust.

— Leverage social media: Social media is a powerful tool for building your personal and professional brand. Utilize platforms like LinkedIn, Twitter, and Instagram to engage with your audience, share your expertise, and promote your brand.

– Network: Building strong relationships with others in your industry and beyond is critical to establishing a strong brand. Attend events, join professional organizations, and seek out opportunities to connect with others who can help you build your reputation and grow your brand.

– Deliver on your promises: Your brand is only as strong as your ability to deliver on your promises. Make sure that your products and services are of high quality, and that you are providing value and solving problems for your target audience.

– Seek feedback and measure results: Regularly seek feedback from your audience, customers, and peers, and measure the results of your branding efforts. This will help you identify areas for improvement and ensure that you are on track to building a strong and successful brand.

By following these strategies and techniques, you can build a strong personal and professional reputation that sets you apart from the competition and helps you achieve success in all areas of your life. Remember, branding is an ongoing process – it's not something you do once and forget about. Keep refining and improving your brand, and never stop seeking out opportunities to grow and expand your reputation. With dedication and persistence, you can build a strong brand that helps you unleash your potential and achieve your goals.

30: Presentation Skills: Communicating Your Ideas with Confidence

Presentation skills are critical for success in both personal and professional settings. Whether you're giving a speech, leading a meeting, or simply trying to persuade someone to see your point of view, the ability to communicate your ideas effectively and with confidence can make all the difference. Here are some proven strategies and techniques for improving your presentation skills and making a powerful impact:

– Know your audience: Before you begin preparing your presentation, it's important to understand who your audience is and what they care about. What are their needs, interests, and goals? This information will help you tailor your message and ensure that your presentation is relevant and engaging.

– Plan and organize your presentation: Effective presentations start with a clear and well-organized structure. Create an outline of your main points, and consider using visual aids like slides or props to help illustrate your ideas.

30: PRESENTATION SKILLS: COMMUNICATING YOUR IDEAS WITH CONFIDENCE

– Prepare your material thoroughly: Take the time to research and gather all the information you need to support your arguments. Ensure that your material is accurate, relevant, and up-to-date.

– Practice your delivery: Rehearse your presentation several times, and pay close attention to your body language, tone of voice, and pacing. Practicing will help you build confidence, iron out any kinks, and ensure that you're delivering your message effectively.

– Engage your audience: A good presentation is not just about delivering information, it's about engaging and inspiring your audience. Use humor, storytelling, and interactive elements like polls or Q&A sessions to keep your audience interested and invested in your message.

– Use visual aids effectively: Visual aids like slides, props, or videos can greatly enhance your presentation, but they must be used effectively to be effective. Avoid overloading your slides with text, and make sure that your visual aids are clear, concise, and easy to understand.

– Be confident and present yourself well: Confidence is key

to giving an effective presentation. Stand up straight, make eye contact, and speak clearly and loudly. Avoid filler words like "um" and "ah," and instead use pauses for emphasis.

– Anticipate questions and be prepared: Be prepared for questions from your audience, and have answers ready for the most likely ones. This will show that you're knowledgeable, confident, and ready to engage with your audience.

– Evaluate your performance: After your presentation, take the time to reflect on your performance and identify areas for improvement. Seek feedback from your audience and consider what you did well and what you could have done better.

By following these strategies and techniques, you can develop the skills and confidence needed to communicate your ideas effectively and make a powerful impact. Remember, presentation skills are not something that you either have or don't have – they're something that you can develop and improve with practice. So be fearless, put yourself out there, and start delivering presentations that inspire and engage your audience. With dedication and persistence, you can unleash your potential and achieve success in all areas of your life.

31: Team Building: Working Together to Achieve Success

Team building is a critical component of success, both in personal and professional settings. By working together effectively, a team can achieve more than the sum of its parts and accomplish incredible things. Here are some proven strategies and techniques for building strong, cohesive teams that can achieve great success:

– Define clear goals and objectives: Teams work best when everyone understands what they're working towards and what their roles and responsibilities are. Clearly define your goals and objectives, and make sure that everyone on the team is aligned and understands what's expected of them.

– Foster open communication: Open, honest communication is the foundation of any strong team. Encourage team members to share their thoughts, ideas, and concerns, and create an environment where everyone feels comfortable expressing themselves.

– Emphasize trust and collaboration: Trust is essential for a team to function effectively. Encourage team members to trust one another, and create opportunities for collaboration and teamwork. This can be achieved through activities like team-building exercises, shared projects, or regular team meetings.

– Recognize and celebrate success: Celebrating success is important for building morale and keeping team members motivated. Recognize and reward the achievements of individuals and the team as a whole, and make sure that everyone feels valued and appreciated.

– Manage conflict effectively: Conflict is inevitable in any team, but it doesn't have to be a negative thing. Teach team members how to manage conflict effectively, and encourage them to resolve disputes through constructive dialogue and problem-solving.

– Foster diversity and inclusiveness: Teams are strongest when they're made up of individuals with a variety of skills, perspectives, and backgrounds. Encourage diversity and inclusiveness, and make sure that everyone on the team feels valued and heard.

– Lead by example: As a team leader, your actions and attitudes set the tone for the entire team. Lead by example, demonstrating integrity, honesty, and respect, and encouraging team members to do the same.

– Encourage personal and professional growth: Teams work best when everyone is growing and developing. Encourage personal and professional growth, and provide opportunities for team members to learn new skills and take on new challenges.

– Evaluate and adjust: Regularly evaluate your team's performance, and make adjustments as necessary. Seek feedback from team members, and use this information to improve processes, resolve conflicts, and increase effectiveness.

By following these strategies and techniques, you can build a strong, cohesive team that is capable of achieving great things. Remember, building a successful team requires effort, dedication, and persistence, but the rewards – increased productivity, enhanced collaboration, and a greater sense of accomplishment – make it all worth it. So gather your team, set your goals, and get started on the road to success, together.

32: Conflict Resolution: Managing Differences and Finding Solutions

Conflict is an inevitable part of life, both in personal and professional settings. Whether it's disagreements between individuals, competing interests, or conflicting priorities, conflicts can arise in any situation. The key to success is learning how to manage these conflicts effectively, and finding solutions that work for everyone involved. Here are some proven strategies and techniques for resolving conflicts and achieving success:

– Identify the root cause of the conflict: Before you can resolve a conflict, it's important to understand what's causing it. Ask questions, listen actively, and try to identify the underlying issues that are fueling the conflict.

– Practice active listening: Active listening is a critical component of effective conflict resolution. Listen to the perspectives and concerns of all parties involved, and make an effort to understand their point of view.

– Stay calm and neutral: Conflicts can be emotionally charged, but it's important to stay calm and neutral in order to resolve them effectively. Avoid getting defensive, and keep your emotions in check.

– Focus on finding common ground: Conflict resolution is about finding a solution that works for everyone involved. Focus on finding common ground, and explore options that are acceptable to all parties.

– Encourage open and honest communication: Open, honest communication is essential for resolving conflicts effectively. Encourage all parties to express their thoughts and feelings, and create an environment where everyone feels comfortable speaking up.

– Be creative and flexible: Conflicts can be complex and challenging, but they can also be an opportunity for creativity and innovation. Be open to new ideas and approaches, and be flexible in your thinking.

– Consider the long-term impact: When resolving conflicts, it's important to consider the long-term impact of your actions. Will the solution you choose create more problems down the road, or will it set the stage for a long-term resolution?

– Seek outside help if needed: If a conflict is particularly complex or difficult to resolve, consider seeking outside help. A neutral third party can help facilitate a resolution and provide an objective perspective.

– Follow up and evaluate: Once a conflict has been resolved, it's important to follow up and evaluate the solution. Ask all parties involved for feedback, and make adjustments as necessary.

By following these strategies and techniques, you can effectively manage conflicts and find solutions that work for everyone involved. Remember, conflict resolution requires patience, empathy, and a willingness to compromise, but the benefits – increased understanding, enhanced relationships, and a greater sense of accomplishment – make it all worth it. So when conflicts arise, stay calm, focus on finding common ground, and work together to find a solution.

33: Diversity and Inclusion: Embracing Differences and Building Strong Teams

Diversity and inclusion are critical components of success in today's world. By embracing differences and building teams that reflect the diversity of our communities, we can tap into the full range of perspectives, skills, and experiences that drive innovation and growth. Here are some proven strategies and techniques for promoting diversity and inclusion in your personal and professional life:

— Embrace diversity: Embrace differences and celebrate the unique perspectives, skills, and experiences that each person brings to the table. Recognize the value of diversity, and make it a priority in your personal and professional life.

— Encourage open and honest communication: Open, honest communication is essential for promoting diversity and inclusion. Encourage all parties to express their thoughts and feelings, and create an environment where everyone feels comfortable speaking up.

— Foster a culture of respect: A culture of respect is essential for promoting diversity and inclusion. Treat everyone with

dignity and respect, and make it clear that all voices are valued and heard.

– Lead by example: As a leader, it's important to lead by example. Model the behaviors and attitudes that you want to
see in your team, and set a positive tone for the organization.

– Promote equality and fairness: Promote equality and fairness in all your interactions and decision-making processes.
Ensure that everyone has equal access to opportunities and
resources, and that your team is free from discrimination
and bias.

– Encourage diversity in hiring and promotion: Encourage
diversity in your hiring and promotion processes, and actively seek out candidates from underrepresented groups.
Make sure that your team reflects the diversity of your community, and that everyone has equal opportunities for success.

– Offer diversity and inclusion training: Offer diversity and
inclusion training for your team, and encourage everyone to
participate. This will help your team understand the im-

portance of diversity and inclusion, and will provide them with the skills and knowledge they need to promote these values in the workplace.

– Celebrate diversity: Celebrate diversity by recognizing the achievements and contributions of all team members, and by creating opportunities for everyone to share their perspectives and experiences.

– Foster a sense of community: Foster a sense of community by encouraging collaboration, teamwork, and mutual support. Work together to build strong, inclusive teams that are able to achieve great things.

By following these strategies and techniques, you can promote diversity and inclusion in your personal and professional life, and build teams that are more resilient, innovative, and successful. Remember, diversity and inclusion are not just the right thing to do, they are essential for building strong, sustainable organizations and communities that thrive. So embrace differences, encourage open communication, and work together to build a world that is more inclusive and equitable for everyone.

34: Change Management: Navigating and Embracing Change

Change is a constant in our lives, and it's often one of the biggest challenges we face. Whether it's a personal change, such as a career transition, or a professional change, such as a reorganization of your company, change can be difficult to navigate and embrace. But by following the right strategies and techniques, you can turn change into a positive and empowering experience. Here are some of the most effective ways to manage change:

– Embrace change: The first step to managing change is to embrace it. Rather than resisting change or fearing the unknown, choose to see it as an opportunity for growth and personal development.

– Prepare for change: Prepare for change by gathering as much information as possible about what's coming. Ask questions, seek advice, and research your options to gain a better understanding of what you're facing.

– Create a plan: Create a plan for managing change, and break it down into manageable steps. Having a clear, actionable plan will help you stay focused and motivated as you navigate the change process.

– Be proactive: Be proactive in managing change, and don't wait for things to happen to you. Take the initiative to create new opportunities and to shape your own future.

– Seek support: Seek support from friends, family, and professional networks as you navigate change. Having a support system in place can provide you with the encouragement and motivation you need to succeed.

– Maintain a positive attitude: Maintain a positive attitude, even in the face of adversity. A positive outlook can help you see the opportunities that are hidden within the change, and will give you the resilience and determination you need to succeed.

– Celebrate successes: Celebrate your successes as you navigate change, and recognize the progress you're making. Celebrating your achievements will help you stay motivated and energized, and will give you the confidence you need to continue on your journey.

– Be flexible: Be flexible and open-minded as you navigate

change. Be willing to try new things, to think outside the box, and to embrace new opportunities.

– Learn from your experiences: Learn from your experiences as you navigate change, and use your newfound knowledge and understanding to grow and develop.

By following these strategies and techniques, you can successfully manage change and turn it into a positive, empowering experience. Remember, change is inevitable, but with the right approach, you can turn it into a valuable opportunity for growth and personal development. So embrace change, prepare for it, and use it as a catalyst for achieving your goals and transforming your life.

35: Legacy: Leaving a Lasting Impact and Inspiring Future Generations

Legacy is about leaving a lasting impact on the world and inspiring future generations. It's about the influence you have on others, the impact you make in your community, and the memories you leave behind. Here are some strategies and techniques for building a lasting legacy:

– Live with purpose: Live with purpose by identifying your values, passions, and goals, and aligning your actions and decisions with them. A life lived with purpose is one that leaves a lasting impact.

– Invest in relationships: Invest in your relationships, both personal and professional, by building deep and meaningful connections with others. Building strong relationships with others will help you create a lasting legacy.

– Give back: Give back to your community by volunteering your time, skills, and resources to help others. By giving back, you'll inspire others to do the same and leave a lasting impact.

35: LEGACY: LEAVING A LASTING IMPACT AND IN-SPIRING FUTURE GENERATIONS

– Share your knowledge: Share your knowledge and expertise with others by mentoring, teaching, and coaching. By passing on your skills and knowledge, you'll inspire future generations to do the same.

– Create something of value: Create something of value, whether it's a business, a book, a piece of art, or a new product. By creating something of value, you'll leave a lasting impact on the world.

– Pursue excellence: Pursue excellence in everything you do by setting high standards, working hard, and constantly striving for improvement. By pursuing excellence, you'll inspire others to do the same.

– Lead by example: Lead by example by embodying the values, beliefs, and behaviors you want to inspire in others. By leading by example, you'll inspire future generations to do the same.

– Celebrate your accomplishments: Celebrate your accomplishments, both big and small, and share your successes with others. By celebrating your achievements, you'll inspire others to do the same.

35: LEGACY: LEAVING A LASTING IMPACT AND IN-SPIRING FUTURE GENERATIONS

– Create a legacy plan: Create a legacy plan by reflecting on your life, your values, and your impact on the world. This plan will help you clarify your goals and focus your efforts on building a lasting legacy.

– Leave a lasting impact: Finally, focus on leaving a lasting impact by making a positive difference in the world, inspiring others to do the same, and leaving a legacy that will be remembered for generations to come.

By following these strategies and techniques, you can build a lasting legacy and inspire future generations to do the same. Remember, legacy is not about the material possessions you leave behind, but about the impact you have on others and the memories you create. So focus on living a purposeful life, investing in relationships, and giving back to your community, and you'll leave a lasting legacy that will inspire future generations.

36: Conclusion: Celebrating Your Success and Continuing Your Journey

Congratulations! You've reached the end of this guide to personal growth and fulfillment, and you should be proud of your progress and achievements so far. As you celebrate your success, it's important to reflect on your journey and consider what's next. Here are some strategies and techniques for celebrating your success and continuing your journey towards success:

− Celebrate your achievements: Celebrate your achievements, both big and small, and acknowledge the hard work and dedication you've put in to get to this point. Take time to reflect on what you've accomplished and how far you've come.

− Reflect on your journey: Reflect on your journey and consider what you've learned, what you would do differently, and what you're proud of. Take time to think about the challenges you've overcome and the lessons you've learned.

− Set new goals: Set new goals for your future, both personal and professional, and make a plan for how you're going to achieve them. Focus on what you want to achieve and what you're going to do to make it happen.

– Celebrate your progress: Celebrate your progress, both big and small, and acknowledge the steps you're taking to achieve your goals. Focus on the positive changes you're making and the progress you're making towards your goals.

– Stay positive: Stay positive and focus on the good in your life. Surround yourself with positive, supportive people, and celebrate your successes and achievements.

– Be grateful: Be grateful for all the good things in your life, including your health, your family, your friends, and your achievements. Focus on what you have, rather than what you don't have.

– Seek out new opportunities: Seek out new opportunities for growth and learning, both personal and professional. Focus on what you can do to improve and grow, and take advantage of opportunities when they arise.

– Stay motivated: Stay motivated by focusing on your goals, and remind yourself of why you're working so hard to achieve them. Surround yourself with positive and supportive people who will encourage you and help you stay motivated.

– Keep learning: Keep learning by seeking out new knowledge and skills, and never stop growing and developing as a person. Focus on what you can do to improve and stay on the path to success.

– Celebrate your success: Finally, celebrate your success and all the hard work and dedication you've put in to get to this point. Celebrate your achievements, reflect on your journey, and focus on what's next.

By following these strategies and techniques, you can celebrate your success and continue your journey towards success. Remember, success is a journey, not a destination, and there is always room for growth and improvement. So focus on celebrating your success, setting new goals, and staying positive, and you'll continue to achieve great things and reach new heights of success.

Thank You

As we reach the end of this book, I want to say thanks for reading this book.

I want to get this information out to as many people as possible. If you found this book helpful, I would greatly appreciate you leaving me a review. This helps others find the book as well.

Disclaimer

This document is geared towards providing exact and reliable information in regards to the topic and issue covered. The publication is sold on the idea that the publisher is not required to render an accounting, officially permitted, or otherwise, qualified services. If advice is necessary, legal, financial, medical or professional, a practiced individual in the profession should be ordered.

This information is not presented by a financial or medical practitioner and is for entertainment, educational and informational purposes only. The content is not intended as a substitute for professional medical advice, diagnosis, or treatment. Always seek the advice of your physician or other qualified health care provider with any questions you may have regarding a medical condition. Never disregard professional medical advice or delay in seeking it because of something you have read.

The information provided herein is stated to be truthful and consistent, in that any liability, in terms of inattention or otherwise, by any usage or abuse of any policies, processes, or directions contained within is the solitary and utter responsibility of the recipient reader. Under no circumstances

DISCLAIMER

will any legal responsibility or blame be held against the publisher for any reparation, damages, or monetary loss due to the information herein, either directly or indirectly.

www.ingramcontent.com/pod-product-compliance
Lightning Source LLC
Chambersburg PA
CBHW060324130626
46553CB00003B/904